Eleanor Roosevelt

Wendy Conklin, M.A.

Publishing Credits

Historical Consultant
Fernando A. Pérez, M.A.Ed.

Editor
Torrey Maloof

Editorial Director
Emily R. Smith, M.A.Ed.

Editor-in-Chief
Sharon Coan, M.S.Ed.

Creative Director
Lee Aucoin

Illustration Manager
Timothy J. Bradley

Publisher
Rachelle Cracchiolo, M.S.Ed.

Teacher Created Materials
5301 Oceanus Drive
Huntington Beach, CA 92649-1030
http://www.tcmpub.com

ISBN 978-0-7439-0667-8

Reprinted 2011
Printed in China

Table of Contents

Great Strides in Society.. 4–5

The Early Years 6–7

Does Mother Know Best?.. 8–9

Tragedy Strikes 10–11

Politics Is Still a Man's Game.................................12–13

The Stock Market Crashes.......................................14–15

Giving the Nation a New Deal.................................16–17

Changing the Role of the First Lady........................18–19

Fighting for Civil Rights..20–21

Helping Marian Anderson..22–23

Just Too Much to Do..24–25

Other Amazing Women 26–29

Glossary.. 30

Index.. 31

Image Credits.. 32

Great Strides in Society

The year of 1920 brought a huge victory for women. After nearly 150 years, women won the right to vote. This act was just the beginning of a new era for women. They would go on to compete in the Olympics in 1928. By the end of the decade, they would hold 39 percent of all college degrees. Women could be doctors and lawyers. Even with these **accomplishments** (uh-KAM-plish-muhnts) many people still wanted women to stay at home.

There was one very important woman who broke all the rules. Early in life, she decided to be true to herself. She fought for equal rights for everyone. She was a writer, speaker, and advisor. She set her own agenda and her own goals as the wife of a president. Her name was Eleanor Roosevelt.

Eleanor Roosevelt delivers a speech.

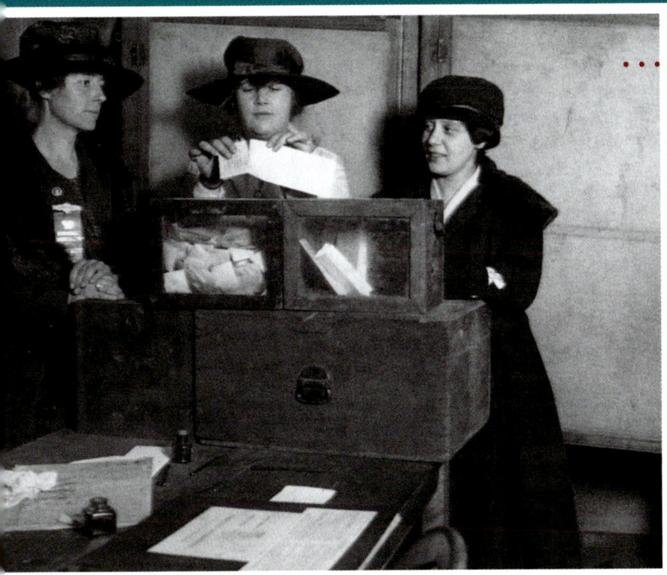

Three proud women cast their first votes in an election.

Sixty-sixth Congress of the United States of America;

At the First Session,

Begun and held at the City of Washington on Monday, the nineteenth day of May, one thousand nine hundred and nineteen.

JOINT RESOLUTION

Proposing an amendment to the Constitution extending the right of suffrage to women.

Resolved by the Senate and House of Representatives of the United States of America in Congress assembled (two-thirds of each House concurring therein), That the following article is proposed as an amendment to the Constitution, which shall be valid to all intents and purposes as part of the Constitution when ratified by the legislatures of three-fourths of the several States.

"ARTICLE ———.

"The right of citizens of the United States to vote shall not be denied or abridged by the United States or by any State on account of sex.

"Congress shall have power to enforce this article by appropriate legislation."

F. H. Gillett

Speaker of the House of Representatives.

Thos. R. Marshall

Vice President of the United States and President of the Senate.

Life in the 1920s

World War I, or the Great War, was over. People were moving on with their lives. For the first time in America, almost everyone could afford cars and radios.

The Nineteenth Amendment

The Nineteenth **Amendment** to the Constitution gave women the right to vote. The right to vote is also called **suffrage** (SUH-fridge).

The Nineteenth Amendment changed the lives of all women in the United States.

The Early Years

Eleanor Roosevelt's life as a child was not a happy one. Her mother felt that it was important to be beautiful. Instead of taking after her mother's good looks, Roosevelt's teeth stuck out. This made her mother ashamed. On the other hand, Roosevelt was the apple of her father's eye. He called her his "miracle from heaven." She loved her father deeply and wanted to please him.

Sadly, at a young age Roosevelt's life suddenly fell apart. Her mother died when she was just eight years old, and two years later her father died. Roosevelt felt terrible about the deaths. She lived with her grandmother. When she was 15 years old, she went to school in Europe.

Going to an all-girl's school changed Roosevelt's life. The **headmistress** (head-MIS-truhs) saw beyond Roosevelt's looks. She knew Roosevelt was smart. This teacher took the time to educate Roosevelt. The girls there learned about politics and poetry. They learned how to think for themselves. Most people did not think this was important for women in the early 1900s.

Traveling the World

Young Eleanor traveled with her headmistress during the summers. They visited Italy and France. It was a great time for this smart young woman.

Famous Family

The Roosevelt family had ancestors who signed the Declaration of Independence in 1776!

The signing of the Declaration of Independence

Eleanor Roosevelt attended a school for girls in England. This image shows a busy street in London about the time that Roosevelt went to school there.

As a young girl, Eleanor loved her father deeply. She is pictured here (on the far right) with her father and two brothers.

Does Mother Know Best?

Eleanor Roosevelt married another Roosevelt. Her husband's name was Franklin Roosevelt. He was Eleanor's fifth cousin. His mother, Sara, was the boss of Eleanor and Franklin's home. She chose where they would live and told them how to raise their children. In fact, she lived in the house right next door. She even had **passageways** built so she could visit whenever she wanted.

In his twenties, Franklin's **political** (puh-LIT-uh-kuhl) career began. He became a state senator in 1910. Three years later, he worked as the assistant secretary of the navy. He even tried to become vice president.

Since Sara ran the Roosevelt household, Eleanor had time to follow her own interests. She even found time to go to business school. She supported women's suffrage. She felt that women were smart enough to have a place in politics. The League of Women Voters believed this, too. So, Eleanor worked with them. She took an interest in Congress and sent them reports. The League of Women Voters soon found that they could not be successful without Eleanor's help.

A group of women register to vote with the help of the League of Women Voters.

Eleanor and Franklin Roosevelt took their honeymoon trip in 1905.

The Supportive Wife

Eleanor Roosevelt knew how to be a politician's wife. She traveled with him, hosted dinners, and met with other politicians. She was one of the keys to her husband's success.

Red Cross, Here I Come!

During World War I, Mrs. Roosevelt worked for the Red Cross. She served meals. She also visited sick soldiers and fought for good health care for all soldiers.

Eleanor Roosevelt worked in soup kitchens to help local communities.

Tragedy Strikes

Life was good for the Roosevelts. It seemed as if nothing could stop Franklin until one day in 1921. Franklin woke up to find he had **polio** (POH-lee-oh). At just 39 years old, he had to face the fact that his life had changed forever. For the first time in his life, Franklin knew what it was like to struggle.

Franklin's mother told him that he should give up politics. But his wife told him to not give up on his dreams. Luckily, Franklin listened to his wife. In later years, Eleanor said that Franklin's illness really proved to be a good thing. It gave him courage and strength that he had not had before. Eleanor knew this from her own tough experiences as a child.

The country was lucky that Franklin listened to his wife. She supported him and kept his name active in politics.

Open for Business

Eleanor and two other friends opened a furniture store. They hired other people to make the furniture. It was very rare for a woman to own a business.

Polio Vaccine

Vaccines (vak-SEENS) are special medicine. These medicines help keep people from getting certain diseases. Polio was a very scary disease in the early 1900s. Starting in the early 1950s, children began receiving an oral polio vaccine in sugar cubes. By 1963, the vaccine was given in shots. Most children still receive this vaccine today.

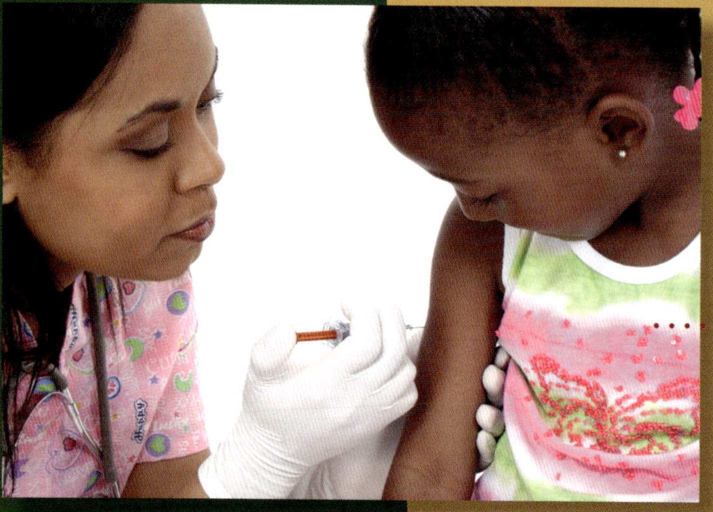

Dr. Jonas Salk invented the polio vaccine in the 1950s. This vaccine has saved many lives.

Politics Is Still a Man's Game

As Franklin worked to regain his strength, Eleanor had something important to do. She worked with the New York State Democratic Party. They had her speak at political **rallies**. She also wrote for the *Women's Democratic News*. The public even heard her on the radio. But Eleanor quickly learned that politics was still a man's arena.

New York let women form their own division of the Democratic Party. But it was the men who ran the party and made the policies. The men did not really care about hearing what the women thought. They made Eleanor wait

Mrs. Roosevelt gets ready for one of her many radio broadcasts.

outside the door of all their important meetings. She never knew if they even read her proposals.

Eleanor worked with others who thought like her. They wanted a 48-hour work week for women and fair wages. They wanted the right to form women's unions. And, of course, they wanted an equal voice with men. Needless to say, Mrs. Roosevelt stayed very busy during this time.

Mr. and Mrs. Roosevelt and their five children: Anna, Elliot, James, Franklin Jr., and John

Buying a School

Eleanor bought an all-girls school in New York. It was called the Todhunter School. She taught literature, drama, and history. She loved every minute of it. Her old headmistress had taught her how to be a good teacher.

The Roosevelt Family

In the middle of all the politics and teaching, Eleanor raised five children.

It's Hoover's Fault!

President Herbert Hoover had only been in office for eight months when the stock market crashed. It did not matter. The public blamed him for its problems.

Black Tuesday

The day the stock market crashed is called Black Tuesday. This is the day the Great Depression really began. Instead of using the word *panic*, Hoover used the term *depression*. It stuck, and now this time is called the Great Depression.

The Stock Market Crashes

Franklin did get back into politics once his health improved. New Yorkers elected him to be their governor in 1929. It looked like this would be a promising year for the Roosevelts. But 1929 was a bad year for the rest of the country.

In the 1920s, people were making quick money. They bought stocks at low prices and sold them at high prices. The problem with this is that they were buying these stocks with credit, not cash. They spent more money than they had in the banks. All this came to a halt on Tuesday, October 29, 1929. This is the day that the New York Stock Exchange crashed.

Families lost their cars and homes. Banks closed. People who had savings accounts lost them. Business owners could not pay their employees. So, people lost their jobs.

President Herbert Hoover did not know how to solve the problems. He thought he could just talk about the good things and the nation would bounce back.

This is Wall Street near the New York Stock Exchange on October 29, 1929.

Giving the Nation a New Deal

By 1932, the country was in bad shape. More than 13 million people were out of work. Banks ran out of cash and went out of business. People did not have enough to eat. They had to visit soup kitchens. The country was in the middle of the Great Depression.

Franklin decided to run for president. He wanted to help the country solve its problems. Franklin said, "I pledge you, I pledge myself, to a new deal for the American people."

Eleanor stopped everything she was doing. Then, she **campaigned** (kam-PAYND) to help him win. In her heart, though, Eleanor did not want to be the First Lady. She knew she would have to give up some of the things she enjoyed most.

The voters thought that Franklin would help farmers, businesses, and people without jobs. So they elected Franklin president in 1932.

Franklin gives a brief speech while on the campaign trail. He promised a new deal to the nation of voters.

What Is Social Security?

Social Security was one program in the New Deal. The government takes a tax out of workers' paychecks. People who are too old or hurt to work get the money. This program helps the older citizens of the country.

Social Security Today

Social Security is still in effect today. But some people worry that soon there will not be enough money. Today, people are living longer. It takes more money to help them. Politicians are trying to solve this problem.

These posters were created by the Work Projects Administration in Ohio. This group was part of the New Deal.

Never Give Up!

In Franklin's inaugural (ih-NAW-gyuh-ruhl) speech, he said, "The only thing you have to fear is fear itself!" By this, he meant Americans had to look fear in the face, keep going, and not give up. This was a lesson both Franklin and Eleanor knew from experience.

Fireside Chats

Franklin talked to the people on the radio. People called these talks Fireside Chats. That's because he had an easy way of speaking. He sounded like he was talking right to each person who listened.

President Roosevelt gives a Fireside Chat.

Changing the Role of the First Lady

Never before had there been a First Lady like Mrs. Roosevelt. She earned her own paycheck giving speeches and writing articles. She met with the press on a regular basis. The First Lady had her own career. No First Lady had ever done those things before!

Even though they did not know her, people felt close to Eleanor. She received thousands of letters asking her for help. Some begged for her old clothes because they did not have any to wear. Others asked her for money to pay their bills. Eleanor tried to help many of these people. But she could not help them all.

President Roosevelt could not travel easily. So, the First Lady was his eyes and ears. She traveled around the country. She visited people firsthand to see how they lived. Eleanor worked in soup kitchens to serve hungry people. She met farmers who had lost their farms. She even sponsored a camp in New York that trained women for jobs. Mrs. Roosevelt did everything she could to help people in America.

Douglas Chandor is known for his oil paintings of great political figures. In 1949, he painted this portrait of Eleanor Roosevelt.

The United Nations adopted the Universal Declaration of Human Rights in 1948. Here, Mrs. Roosevelt holds a copy of this document.

Fighting for Civil Rights

Eleanor wanted equal rights for everyone. After all, is it really a **democracy** (dih-MAW-kruh-see) if people are not treated the same? In the 1930s, many people **discriminated** (dis-KRIM-uh-nate-uhd) against African Americans. This means African Americans were treated unfairly. Eleanor noticed that African Americans did not have the same education as whites. They could not eat at the same restaurants. African Americans did not have the same chances for good jobs either. Some towns even kept them from voting.

As First Lady, she knew she had to do something about this. Eleanor asked some politicians to work for **civil rights**. She joined the board of the National Association for the Advancement of Colored People (NAACP). After she was no longer First Lady, she worked with Martin Luther King Jr. She never gave up fighting for all people to have the same rights.

Eleanor's Views

Some of Eleanor's views on civil rights made Franklin's advisors uneasy. They were afraid that she would hurt his reputation. Many people who supported Franklin did not support Eleanor.

Civil Rights Act of 1964

Eleanor died before the Civil Rights Act of 1964 was passed. This act states that all people in America have the same rights. Eleanor would have been proud of this new law.

H. R. 7152 PUBLIC LAW 88-352

JUL 6 1964
NARS

Eighty-eighth Congress of the United States of America

AT THE SECOND SESSION

Begun and held at the City of Washington on Tuesday, the seventh day of January, one thousand nine hundred and sixty-four

An Act

To enforce the constitutional right to vote, to confer jurisdiction upon the district courts of the United States to provide injunctive relief against discrimination in public accommodations, to authorize the Attorney General to institute suits to protect constitutional rights in public facilities and public education, to extend the Commission on Civil Rights, to prevent discrimination in federally assisted programs, to establish a Commission on Equal Employment Opportunity, and for other purposes.

Be it enacted by the Senate and House of Representatives of the United States of America in Congress assembled, That this Act may be cited as the "Civil Rights Act of 1964".

TITLE I—VOTING RIGHTS

SEC. 101. Section 2004 of the Revised Statutes (42 U.S.C. 1971), as amended by section 131 of the Civil Rights Act of 1957 (71 Stat. 637), and as further amended by section 601 of the Civil Rights Act of 1960 (74 Stat. 90), is further amended as follows:

(a) Insert "1" after "(a)" in subsection (a) and add at the end of subsection (a) the following new paragraphs:

"(2) No person acting under color of law shall—

"(A) in determining whether any individual is qualified under State law or laws to vote in any Federal election, apply any standard, practice, or procedure different from the standards, practices, or procedures applied under such law or laws to other individuals within the same county, parish, or similar political subdivision who have been found by State officials to be qualified to vote;

"(B) deny the right of any individual to vote in any Federal election because of an error or omission on any record or paper relating to any application, registration, or other act requisite to voting, if such error or omission is not material in determining whether such individual is qualified under State law to vote in such election; or

"(C) employ any literacy test as a qualification for voting in any Federal election unless (i) such test is administered to each individual and is conducted wholly in writing, and (ii) a certified copy of the test and of the answers given by the individual is furnished to him within twenty-five days of the submission of his request made within the period of time during which records and papers are required to be retained and preserved pursuant to title III of the Civil Rights Act of 1960 (42 U.S.C. 1974–74e; 74 Stat. 88): *Provided, however*, That the Attorney General may enter into agreements with appropriate State or local authorities that preparation, conduct, and maintenance of such tests in accordance with the provisions of applicable State or local law, including such special provisions as are necessary in the preparation, conduct, and maintenance of such tests for persons who are blind or otherwise physically handicapped, meet the purposes of this subparagraph and constitute compliance therewith.

"(3) For purposes of this subsection—

"(A) the term 'vote' shall have the same meaning as in subsection (e) of this section;

"(B) the phrase 'literacy test' includes any test of the ability to read, write, understand, or interpret any matter."

(b) Insert immediately following the period at the end of the first sentence of subsection (c) the following new sentence: "If in any such proceeding literacy is a relevant fact there shall be a rebuttable

The Civil Rights Act of 1964

Helping Marian Anderson

Marian Anderson was a well-known singer during the 1930s. She had an amazing voice and was an instant success.

Anderson planned to sing at a popular location in Washington, D.C. She was told she could not sing there because she was African American. It did not matter to them that she was a great artist.

Making a Big Statement

The Lincoln Memorial was built to honor Abraham Lincoln. He was the president who freed the slaves. He fought for equality for all. It was the perfect place for Anderson to sing. It made a big statement.

Daughters of the Revolution

It was the Daughters of the American Revolution who **banned** Anderson from singing. Eleanor was a member of this important group. Right away, she sent a letter resigning her membership. This was a big blow to the group. No one wanted to make the first lady mad!

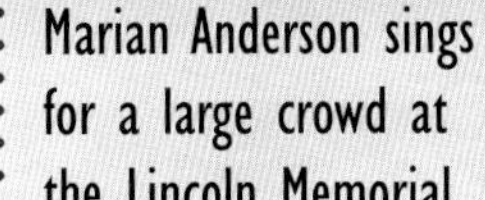
Marian Anderson sings for a large crowd at the Lincoln Memorial.

Eleanor Roosevelt was furious about this. She knew this was wrong. So, the First Lady figured out a way for Anderson to sing somewhere else in Washington, D.C. This special place was the Lincoln Memorial. Anderson agreed, although she was very nervous. In 1939, she sang to more than 75,000 people. Many more people heard her on the radio.

Anderson's performance ended with the song "America." One line in that song says, "From every mountain side, let freedom ring." It was a very special moment for everyone there.

Eleanor Roosevelt visits a U.S. soldier who was wounded during World War II.

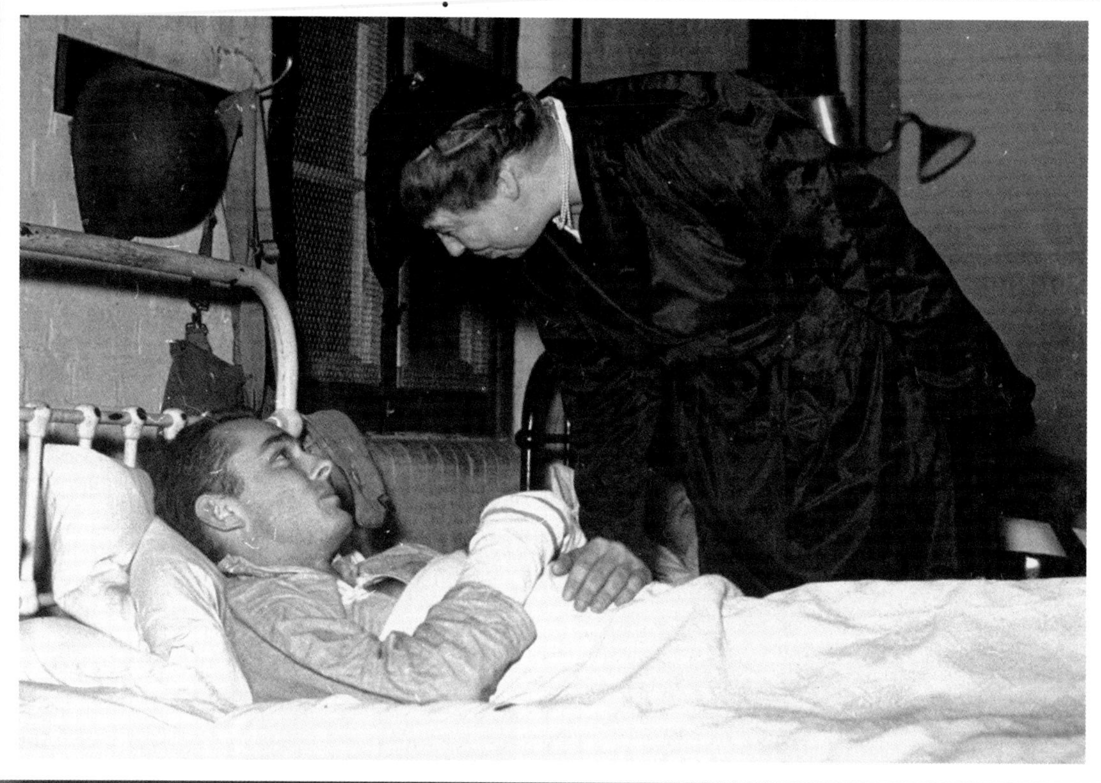

Just Too Much to Do

Franklin and Eleanor were helping the United States deal with hard times during the Great Depression. Others in the world were fighting a war. December 7, 1941, seemed like any other day. But on that day, Japan attacked American soil. Their target was a place called Pearl Harbor. This was a United States military base in Hawaii. Fire and smoke spread, and more than 2,400 people died that day. The president asked Congress to declare war on Japan. Soon after, the nation was at war with Germany, too.

Eleanor's role as First Lady changed again. Now, she was traveling to Europe to see the war-torn areas. She ate with soldiers and took time to visit wounded men.

Just before the war ended, President Roosevelt died. It was a hard time for Eleanor. Her friends wanted her to run for a political office, but she was not interested.

In 1961, she had one last important job. President John F. Kennedy asked her to lead the Commission on the Status of Women. He wanted to know if the workplace treated women fairly.

Eleanor died in 1962. The nation lost an amazing woman. She was the most active First Lady of that time. And, the people lost a defender of civil rights for all.

President John F. Kennedy and Eleanor Roosevelt in 1961

The United Nations

Shortly after Franklin died, Eleanor served as a delegate to the United Nations. It was there that she helped get the Universal Declaration of Human Rights passed. She wanted everyone to have the same freedoms that she had.

Did You Know?

During 1959 and 1960, John Kennedy wrote letters to Eleanor Roosevelt. He was running for president, and he wanted her support. She did not want to support him. She believed that another candidate would make a better president. Kennedy did not want to give up. He knew her opinion was still important to America's voters.

Clara Bow

Clara Bow was an actress. She acted in silent films. These are movies with no sound. By 1930, she had made over 50 movies.

A Gift for the Capitol

Jeannette Rankin's home state was Montana. Leaders of the state donated a bronze statue of Rankin to the U.S. Capitol collection. This statue honors her achievements as a U.S. congresswoman.

Jeannette Rankin

Eleanor Roosevelt was the first wife of a president to fly in an airplane.

Amelia Earhart arrives in Ireland after flying across the Atlantic Ocean alone.

Other Amazing Women

There were other great women who lived during the same time as Eleanor Roosevelt. Each of them made an amazing mark on history, too.

Amelia Earhart was the first woman to fly across the Atlantic Ocean alone. She once flew Mrs. Roosevelt over Washington, D.C. She had a dream to be the first woman to fly around the world. Unfortunately, on her trip around the world, Earhart's plane went missing. It was never found.

In 1916, Jeannette Rankin was the first woman elected to Congress. This was before women could even vote! She brought up the debate on women's voting rights in Congress. Thanks in part to her work, the Nineteenth Amendment passed. She ran for Congress again in 1939 and won. She was the only member of Congress to vote against declaring war on Japan in 1941.

Other Amazing Women *(cont.)*

There was a branch of the army that was just for women during World War II. These were the first female soldiers. Colonel Mary Hallaren commanded the Women's Army Corps. She paved the way for women to fight in combat.

Thanks to Dorothea Lange, people today know what life was like in the Great Depression. It was her camera that told the stories of the **migrants**. When others saw the pictures, they offered help to these poor workers. During World War II, she took pictures of **Japanese internment camps**. The nation was shocked to see the awful conditions the people lived in. Today, these powerful photographs are in museums.

In the 1990s, Hallaren helped create the Women's Memorial at Arlington National Cemetery.

Lange's photographs make the Great Depression real to people today.

In 1991, Anderson received a Grammy® Lifetime Achievement Award.

Eleanor Roosevelt and these other amazing women made life richer for women today. They stood up for what they believed and fought battles to make American dreams come true for everyone. Their work in the past has ensured freedom for women, and other minorities, today and in the future.

Anderson at the Opera

Marian Anderson was the first African American member of the New York Metropolitan Opera.

Famous Writers, Too

Gertrude Stein was a famous author of this time. She was well respected by other artists. Virginia Woolf is another well-known female author. These women opened the world of literature to female authors.

Glossary

accomplishments—achievements of goals

amendment—a change made to the Constitution; two-thirds of the states must agree to the change

banned—kept from or excluded

campaigned—sought votes for a candidate who ran for office

civil rights—the rights and freedoms that people are given in the Constitution

democracy—a government system where the people elect the leaders

discriminated—to be treated unfairly because of race, gender, or something similar

headmistress—the title of a woman who is the leader or principal of a school

inaugural—relating to when a president takes office

Japanese internment camps—places where Japanese American citizens were taken and kept during World War II after the bombing of Pearl Harbor

migrants—people who have moved from one region to another

passageways—hallways that connect from one place to another

polio—a virus that affects nerve cells in the spinal cord and may cause paralysis

political—having to do with politics in government

rallies—an organized meeting where people who believe in something come together to talk about it

suffrage—the right to vote

vaccines—special medicine given to prevent diseases

Index

African Americans, 20, 22–23, 29
"America," 23
Anderson, Marian, 22–23, 29
Arlington National Cemetery, 28
Black Tuesday, 14
Bow, Clara, 26
civil rights, 20–21, 25
Civil Rights Act, 21
Commission on the Status of Women, 25
Congress, 8, 24, 27
Daughters of the American Revolution, 22
Declaration of Independence, 6
Earhart, Amelia, 27
England, 7
Europe, 6, 24
Germany, 24
Great Depression, 14, 16, 24, 28
Hallaren, Mary, 28
Hawaii, 24
Hoover, Herbert, 14
Japan, 24, 27
Japanese internment camps, 28
Kennedy, John F., 25
King, Martin Luther, Jr., 21
Lange, Dorothea, 28
League of Women Voters, 8
Lincoln, Abraham, 22
Lincoln Memorial, 22–23
NAACP, 21
New Deal, 16–17
New York, 12–15, 18
New York Metropolitan Opera, 29
New York State Democratic Party, 12
New York Stock Exchange, 14–15
Nineteenth Amendment, 5, 27
Olympics, 4
Pearl Harbor, 24
polio, 10
Rankin, Jeannette, 26–27
Red Cross, 9
Roosevelt, Anna, 13
Roosevelt, Eliot, 13
Roosevelt, Franklin, 8–14, 16, 18, 21, 24–25
Roosevelt, Franklin Jr., 13
Roosevelt, James, 13
Roosevelt, John, 13
Roosevelt, Sara, 8
Salk, Jonas, 10
Stein, Gertrude, 29
social security, 17
stock market, 14–15
Todhunter School, 13
United Nations, 20, 25
Universal Declaration of Human Rights, 20, 25
Wall Street, 14–15
Washington, D.C., 22–23, 27
Women's Army Corps, 28
Women's Democratic News, 12
Women's Memorial, 28
Woolf, Virginia, 29
World War I, 5, 9
World War II, 24, 28
Work Projects Administration, 17

Image Credits

cover Stock Montage/SuperStock; p.1 Stock Montage/SuperStock; p.4 The Library of Congress; p.5 (top) The Library of Congress; p.5 (bottom) The National Archives; p.6 The Library of Congress; p.7 (top) The Library of Congress; p.7 (bottom) Bettmann/Corbis; pp.8–9 (top) The Granger Collection, New York; pp.8–9 (bottom) Minnesota Historical Society/Corbis; p.9 The Granger Collection, New York; p.10 Jaimie Duplass/Shutterstock, Inc.; p.11 The Granger Collection, New York; p.12 The Granger Collection, New York; p.13 Bachrach/Keystone/Getty Images; p.14 The Library of Congress; p.15 Bettmann/Corbis; p.16 The Library of Congress; p.17 (top) The Library of Congress; p.17 (bottom) The Library of Congress; p.18 Franklin D. Roosevelt Library; p.19 The Granger Collection, New York; p.20 The Granger Collection, New York; p.21 The National Archives; p.22–23 The Library of Congress; p.23 Hulton Archive/Getty Images; p.24 David E. Scherman/Time & Life Pictures/ Getty Images; p.25 Bettmann/Corbis; p.26 (left) The Library of Congress; p.26 (right) The Granger Collection, New York; pp.26–27 The Granger Collection, New York; p.28 (left) The Library of Congress; p.28 (right) The Granger Collection, New York; p.29 The Library of Congress